What's your name? _____

*Draw a face showing how you feel
about meeting new friends.*

The following professionals contributed to this publication:
Sylvia Allinger, Shelly Borchardt, Brian Bradshaw, Gloria Dayley, Theresa Gallardo,
Kathryn Goetz, Gary Harness, Patricia Hauman, M. Kashman,
Carrol Kass, Nancy Kropf, Cynthia Lum, Laurel McCarter, Dr. John Mokkosian,
Alison Morrow, Judith Rae, Rebecca Reynolds, Beth Thompson.

Artist: Tony Vechio

Kim, Carlos and I haven't always been friends.
Kim used to be shy and spent most of her time alone.
I thought she was stuck-up.
Carlos was a new kid in school and the
other kids made fun of the way he talked.

Why is it sometimes hard to make friends?

_____

_____

_____

One day Kim asked me how I made so many friends. I told her I play with lots of kids, but have only a few close friends.

Kim said she would like to have some good friends.

Give three reasons for having friends.

1) _____

2) _____

3) _____

We talked about when and where Kim could meet friends. I suggested she hang out wherever kids get together, like on the school ground before and after school or in her neighborhood on weekends.

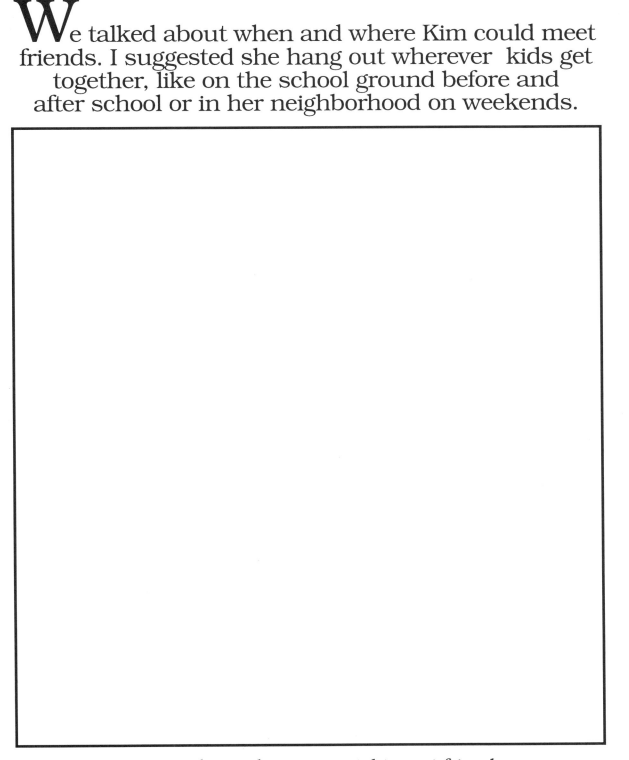

Draw a place where you might meet friends.

When Kim asked how to meet friends, I suggested she start by smiling, saying her name and inviting other kids to play with her. Kim can let other kids know that she cares by sharing something with them or calling them on the phone. She won't meet friends by sitting at home alone all the time.

Write three sentences you might use to meet someone new.

1) Hello, my name is _____.

What's your _____?

2) Hello, my name is _____.

Would you like to _____?

3) Hello, my name is _____.

Can I _____?

Draw a face showing how you will look when you say "hello."

Some kids won't want to be friends with Kim and that can hurt. The best thing is for her to forget about it and find someone who <u>is</u> friendly.

That's just what Kim did.

Tell about how you felt when you tried to be friends and it didn't work .

_____

_____

_____

Carlos noticed that Kim was making friends
and asked me what I had told her.
This is the list I made up for Carlos.

HOW TO MAKE FRIENDS

Go where kids are doing the things you like to do.

*Smile and introduce yourself,
or have someone else introduce you.*

Talk in a friendly voice.

Say things that make the other kid feel good.

*Don't be discouraged if some kids aren't friendly.
Keep trying.*

*Show interest in what the other kid likes,
does and feels.*

Let the other kid tell you about himself or herself.

Tell about yourself, but don't brag or talk too much.

Invite other kids to your house or to play with you.

Share your things with other kids.

Call other kids on the telephone.

*Be yourself,
not what you think others want you to be.*

Carlos said that he had been dreaming of having some good friends to hang out with. I asked him what he was good at.

Carlos said he was a good soccer player.

Name something that keeps you from making friends and what you can do about it.

_____

_____

_____

I invited Carlos to play soccer with me and my friends. He was great. Now all the kids want him on their team. He has made lots of friends.

Give three reasons other kids would want to be friends with you.

1) _____

2) _____

3) _____

When I was sick at home for a week, Kim and Carlos came to visit me. They brought videos for me to watch so I wouldn't be bored. It felt good to have friends that cared.

Tell about a time you felt lonely and wanted a friend.

_____

_____

_____

Some kids told me Kim was saying mean things about me while I was sick. Instead of getting mad, I talked it over with her. We learned that the kids had made up the story to break up our friendship. I trust Kim as my friend.

Who is someone you trust never to hurt you on purpose?

_____

How can you show others that they can trust you? _____

_____

Kim, Carlos and I were together all the time. The more we were together, the more we wanted to be together.

My mom called us "three peas in a pod."

What are some things you like to do with your friends?

After a few months of that, I started getting bored. I wanted to hang out with some other kids too. When I realized that Kim and Carlos didn't want me to have other friends, I knew our friendship had to change.

Tell about how it feels to lose a friend.

I gently told Kim and Carlos that I wanted to spend time with some other kids. I still liked them and wanted to be friends, but needed more time to be with other kids.

What are three gentle ways you can cool a friendship.

1) _____

2) _____

3) _____

A few weeks later an older girl, Rosie, invited me to go to the mall. I asked Kim and Carlos to come with us, but they said they were busy. I thought their feelings were hurt because I wanted to be with Rosie.

What are three things Kim and Carlos can do to feel better.

1)_____

2)_____

3)_____

When Kim and Carlos called after that,
I said I was busy. Soon they stopped calling.
Rosie said I was better off without them.

What can you do if some of your friends don't like each other?

_____

_____

_____

Rosie and I started going to the mall every day after school. She introduced me to her friends and we all hung out together. They were much more exciting then Kim and Carlos. I learned a lot from them.

What are some qualities and interests you look for in a friend?

_____

_____

_____

Rosie called Kim and Carlos "those stupid foreigners." Then she would imitate Carlos talking in broken English and her friends would laugh. I didn't say anything because I didn't want Rosie to make fun of me.

Why do people often make fun of other people who are different?

_____

_____

_____

One day Rosie pulled a mean trick on Kim by hiding her books. This was tough on me. If I told Kim where her books were hidden, Rosie would be mad. Maybe she wouldn't be my friend anymore.

What would you do if you were Vanessa?

_____

_____

_____

Kim asked me if I knew where her books were hidden and I told her "no." Then I felt sick at my stomach. I knew I had lied and broken our friendship. Kim would never trust me again.

How would you feel if a friend turned against you?

_____

_____

_____

Mom told me to stay away from Rosie before she got me into trouble. I figured I was old enough to pick my own friends.

What would you do if your parents told you to stay away from one of your friends?

_____

_____

Later I watched Rosie slip candy and gum in her pockets as we walked through the market. She said the store would never miss them.

What would you do if your friends started stealing?

_____

_____

_____

One day I told Rosie that if she was going to steal, I didn't want to be her friend. She laughed and called me "chicken." I felt hurt and angry.

Tell about a time you said "no" when your friends wanted you to do something wrong.

_____

_____

That night I got a phone call that Rosie and her friends had been caught stealing. That scared me good because I could have been with them. Mom was right. Bad friends lead to big trouble.

How can you tell which friends to stay away from?

_____

_____

_____

After Rosie was arrested, most of the kids quit playing with me. Their folks said if I had been hanging out with kids that stole, I must be a thief too. People are judged by the friends they have.

How do you feel about hanging out with kids that get into trouble?

_____

_____

_____

I told Carlos and Kim that I was sorry for not returning their calls. Kim smiled and took my hand while Carlos told one of his crazy jokes. Good friends know how to forgive each other when they make mistakes.

Tell about a time you forgave a friend for hurting you.

_____

_____

_____

Just because we are friends, that doesn't mean we don't get into arguments. One time we didn't talk to each other for three days. Friends don't have to agree all the time or hide their true feelings.

Tell about a time you made up with a friend after an argument.

_____

_____

_____

Although Carlos, Kim and I fight among ourselves, we stick up for each other. When some kids called Carlos stupid for the way he talks, I told them they were jealous because they only speak one language and he speaks two.

Tell about a time you stuck up for a friend. How did that feel?

_____

_____

_____

Today I have some friends who play sports and others who listen to music. I like to do both of these things. Still, these friendships are different from my relationship with Kim and Carlos. They don't last as long or go as deep.

How have your friendships changed as you have grown older?

_____

_____

_____

Even when I am with other kids, Kim and Carlos know that they are still my closest friends. When we have problems, we are always there for each other. I trust them to keep my deepest secrets.

Who do you talk to about your feelings?

_____

_____

_____

C
arlos, Kim and I have been together through good times and bad. That makes our friendship strong. I hope we can always be together.

Name two people you would like to have for close friends.

1)_____

2)_____

NOTE: This story continues in the book *HOW I FEEL,* which examines the feelings of these three friends when Carlos has to move away.

FREE CATALOG (800) 238-8433